A POETIC EXPRESSION OF OPINIONS RANTS AND OTHER FIGHTING WORDS

I KNOW THIS IS SUCH
AN UNEXPECTED
ARRIVAL,
BUT I COME FOR YOUR
SURVIVAL.
YOU'VE BEEN
SUFFERING WAY TOO
LONG,

I COME TO REVIVE
YOU.

"POETRY IS DEAD"?

WHO SAYS?

BE PATIENT.

YA'LL ACTING LIKE THE POET IS
NONEXISTENT.

LIKE, WE AREN'T RESILIENT.

LIKE, WE CAN'T RAISE THE DEAD.

WHO ELSE CAN JUMP OFF THE LEDGE,
FLY,
AND LAND IN A ROSEBED?

WE PLANT SEEDS,

ALWAYS MAKING SURE THE HOPELESS AND
ROMANTICS ARE INSPIRATIONALLY FED.

ARTiculately Relaying Thoughts

(A R T)

This is just creative venting.

My emotions and opinions,

wishes and visions,

transferred soulfully

onto a blank canvas.

She was all over the place.

Confusion and chaos.

He liked to be caught up in her tornado.

He was tired of normalcy.

He wanted adventure.

She took him to undiscovered worlds.

He was happy just exploring the back of her mind.

THIS IS ALL NOTHING

BUT AN ORGANIZED MESS.

TURNING LETTERS INTO WORDS.

WORDS INTO SENTENCES.

SENTENCES INTO POETRY

AND HOPING FOR THE BEST.

FALSEHOOD

SHE'S STUCK IN A SOCIETY
THAT SEEMS TO OFFER HER
NOTHING BUT DISAPPOINTMENTS.

ILLUSIONS, CONFUSIONS AND
RULES THAT COMPLETELY DEFY
UNIVERSAL LAW;
SHE'S EXPECTED TO UPHOLD.

BELIEVE ME WHEN I TELL YOU
SHE'S DOING THE BEST SHE CAN.

HER RAGE IS AT THE BRIM
AND IT'S TAKING EVERYTHING IN
HER
TO KEEP IT FROM SPILLING.

STAY WOKE

If you're not aware, society will have you losing the very uniqueness you were born with to change the world.

In Purgatory

FEAR

A paralyzing agent produced by the mind

to keep you forever looking up at

dreams suspended over your head

that you will never be able to touch.

DARK SIDE

YOU'VE UPSET
MY SOUL

INTERRUPTED MY
DEMONS FROM
THEIR SLEEPING

KILLING ME
WITH MY OWN
KINDNESS

IM TIRED ,
IVE EXHAUSTED
ALL MY MERCY
ON THIS

THIS IS MORE THAN ,
MERE ANGER

THIS IS
A
CAPRICORNS REVEVENGE

A FEW GOOD LIES

Nah,
You can't handle the truth,
especially not the whole truth.
That shit'll take you to a place
you'll be forced to enter in
involuntarily.
You'll be scared to open doors.
You'll get lost in winding
hallways.
You'll look for windows to jump
out of trying to escape the truth.

Nah,
You ain't ready to welcome
yourself to a house of horrors.
Far from ready to find out you
know absolutely nothing.
You won't be able to fathom it.
Your precious world would
collapse right under your feet for
you to see you've been living in a
bottomless pit of lies and enjoying
it.
You want the truth but you can't
handle the responsibility that
accompanies it.
So hold on to those few good lies
for now.

ORDERED CHAOS

I'm searching for extremes.

Radical changes and rebellion.

Disruption in the midst of order.

Revolutionized tradition

03:00

Wrote some of these verses at
3 am.
I was up before the birds sung
praises to the sun because I
couldn't hold it in.
I had to transfer the anger.
I had to decorate the page with
pain.
I had to let the ink represent my
tears.
3 am soul baring
3 am wall staring

3 am I'm wondering if I still caring
about the things I should still care
about.
Hurt, and it's a heavy amount.
I carried it in my heart and even
though I had a voracious appetite
for love I felt severely starved.
So 3 am I'm writing these thoughts
that would otherwise bury me
underneath the sheets for a week
again.
Now it's 6 am
Now I'll sleep till 3 pm.

ADVOCATUS DIABOLI

LATELY,
I'VE BEEN ON THE FENCE
ABOUT MY SINS.
ASKING MYSELF
WERE THEY TRULY ACTS OF EVIL
OR
UNDOUBTEDLY NEEDED
COMMITTING?

TrAv3ll3r

You may be trying to get back to a
place you once knew in another
lifetime,
my dear nomadic soul.

Maybe that's why you can't seem to
rest and be at peace,
Because no where here feels like
home.

VOID

It wasn't hugs and kisses that I
needed from anyone.
I wasn't daily reassurances.

It was me being able to capture
my pain and develop it through
keystrokes.

It was visions of me transforming,
evolving into something real.

I wasn't looking for attention like
I thought.

It was Me needing to be attentive
to my thoughts.

I was looking for lasting
impressions.

Not interested in chocolates and
timepieces

I wanted a piece of time I
created:
brushstrokes, verses and
arrangements.

I heard love existed so I needed proof.

Kisses weren't good enough
Handholding wasn't convincing enough
Sharing milkshakes and spaghetti
plates didn't look real enough.

I needed something of cosmic worth.
I was looking for something
unclassifiable.

I needed cinematic daydreams
I needed the 9th wonder.

I needed creations I didn't understand.

STRIKE OUTS

IT FELT LIKE
SHE KEPT FAILING AT
TRYING TO MAKE IT
RIGHT.

BROKEN HALOS

YALL HAVE FOOLISHLY
MISUNDERSTOOD
THE THE ANGELS HERE ON
EARTH

Come into MY world.

Everything you need is attainable here.

Wildest dreams are reality here.

Mysteries are fathomed here.

Deep, is explored here.

Life, is lived here.

So yeah, wake up, wake up.

Drink up, drink up, the potion in my cup.

Siphon out the kool-aid in your blood.

All you need is to be yourself to heal up.

KaRmA JOnEs

Legend has it........
If he didn't look at her with lust and
pain in his eyes,
Kissed her passionately with a
mouth full of lies,
Infiltrated her mind with
masculine pride,
and
take her body savagely in the heat
of the night...
She wouldn't take him seriously.

SHOULD I BE
DREAM CHASING
OR
RACING MY
DREAMS
AGAINST MY
FEARS

☆☆☆

RePAIrs AnD COrRecTIOnS

I poured ink
on the wounds
and they turned
into healing words

LATE NIGHT COMPOSITIONS

I'VE WRITTEN A BLUES
SONG WITH NOTHING
BUT
TEARDROPS AND 5
SHOTS.

I stopped questioning certain
things.
I know longer demand they
make sense.

Hmmmmm...

Who knows,
Maybe that's insanity creeping
in.

Well, you know what
I'm ready for that ride,

I am poetically made.
So eloquently constructed
like a verse from Hafiz
I orchestrate these words
with ease.
Salam,
I'm trying to connect with Rumi
I'm rising,
writing poetic prescriptions
for your mental afflictions
like Dr. Angelou.
Dropping jewels,
offering tools to use.
That's what I'm giving you.

a CaPellA

I spit these words with no assistance
other than...
-the beat of my heart.

No ivory keys
But
Having the blues can offer a nice tune

And that

-twinkle of hope in my eye
Is always a nice surprise
Just a soft noise but it's heard the most.

Cus' these verses on their own produce a rhythm
and form a melody if you listen correctly.

This is the first instrument.
The voice..
On its own.

She is a portal to another dimension.
She's magical, for she is mysterious.
Many men curious of what she could be
but he knew some of what she was
and yet he still didn't know of her divinity.
Her kiss to the forehead,
so soothing
Her touch,
so reassuring.
Her eyes,
luring.
Her temple,
Alluring.
This woman was foreign.
She was continually evolving.
Her mind was sharp,
But it couldn't compare to her tongue,
and when the two worked together
thoughts spoken became prophesies...
This was his reality with the midnight queen.
She was the embodiment of all his desires.
His entire body, mind, soul longed for her
Her absence was a trap.
It is a bittersweet experience.
The expectancy of her return was lik
e a long waited coming attraction.
And the solitude it left him with,
excruciating.

OH HOW
STRANGELY
LIBERATING IT HAS
BEEN
TO HAVE FALLEN
INTO THE PLACE OF
THE SUNKEN

☆☆☆

Many survive by praying to Jesus
I've survived by sleeping with my demons.
A romantic with my vices.
Excuse me for my indulgence,
I've got reasons.
I've got a season's pass
for this emotional rollercoaster
so I'm riding with my feelings.
These empty spirit bottles clinking,
I'm sinking
deeper into these wrong decisions
and leaving all my second thoughts
in a place I don't dare go tonight.
So I undress my demons,
And throw all my fraudulent high self esteem out the window.
Nothings in limbo now.

WRONG TYP3

GOT CAUGHT UP IN "TYPES" BASED ON SUPERFICIALITIES, AND GOT CAUGHT UP IN ALL TYPES OF BULLSHIT.

WHAT STRANGE TIMES
WE'RE LIVING IN.
I NEVER THOUGHT IN MY
LIFETIME I'D BE
WITNESSING THE
HAND OF GOD
ON OUR NECKS LIKE
THIS.

NEVER

Will

I

Ever

Again

Look at life through the eyes of those who've never looked life right in the eye.

LA COMMEDIA

SITS ON FLOOR
LIGHTS BLUNT
INHALES
EXHALES
INHALES
EXHALES
INHALES
EXHALES
LAUGHS
LAUGHS
LAUGHS
LOOKS UP
LIFE, WHAT THE HELL?
INHALES
EXHALES
LAUGHS
THROWS BLUNT INTO GASOLINE.

THE END.

No, no, no darling...

Don't look too long.

she'll end up in your dreams...

And that'll only give you

nightmares when you wake.

ScRipT3d HeArt6Re@k

She fears that if she falls in love
the director will say
cut,
wrap it up.
Everyone will exit stage left
and that will be the
end of scene once again.

11:10 PM

Guilt and wine
mixing in my system
Bedtime cocktails
inducing visions

Numb

Feeling everything deeply
The beginning of it all.

"I hate you."
She yelled

And I could tell
by his face..
That hit harder
than any pain he's ever felt
And
Stronger than any love he's ever
known.

EX3CUTIONS

DON'T LET ANYONE'S FAKE

"I LOVE YOU'S"

BE THE GUN
YOU HOLD TO YOUR OWN HEAD.

WMD'S

DESTRUCTIVE CRITICISMS
INSULTS
PSYCHOLOGICAL ABUSE
EMOTIONAL ABUSE
PHYSICAL ABUSE
SPIRITUAL ABUSE

They say one day
you'll be able to look back
on the past and laugh...

I hope so

I can sure use some
comedic relief right about
now.

☆☆☆

Visions of a SPACESHIP

I'm trying to go somewhere,
Somewhere dimensionally different.
Somewhere only the poet can illustrate.
Vivid pictures painted by words birthed
from my lips, giving you an indescribable
outer body experience.
I'm trying to go to a place where whatever
you need is at arm's length
And your wants are right next door offering
so much more.
Somewhere, where the people you really
love, love unconditionally
And the one who is the one loves you
undeniably.
A place where life encourages living.
A place where your dreams and reality
strike up a romance and marry.
Yeah, I'm trying to go there.

It'll ALL starts
making sense
when
it starts making
no sense.

THIS THAT SHIT
THAT GETS YOU
LIFTED
LIKE THAT PURE
WHITE SHIT THAT
GETS YOU
ADDICTED.
I'M YOUR DEALER
PUSHING IT IN YA
SYSTEM

One day I just broke down and asked..

"What do I do?
Seems like I'm not doing anything right.
Somebody tell me what to do."

And no one around me said anything.
They just stared at me.

No one had anything to say.
I couldn't believe it.

but any other time.......

I'M NOT SORRY.
SOME PEOPLE I HAD TO FORCE FEED
HARD TO SWALLOW PILLS
AND WATCH THEM CHOKE.

DEATH TO EGO.

They say
at a certain point
your life should be in
"order".

I laugh out loud at that.

Life throws you so many
unexpectations.

Best you order a round of shots,
dance with chaos; and when joy
comes, romance it like a first
love.

Seems like they've tried to
redesign the woman
to a
man's "liking"
so much that
many woman
don't even
like themselves now.

"What's your name?"

Stop, you don't want to fall in love with a girl like me.

"Why?"

Thunderstorms and tornadoes baby, thunderstorms and tornadoes.

"A man like me knows how to weather storms, tornadoes and hurricanes."

"You won't come out on the other side the same."

" Well, if that's the price I gotta pay..."

Trust me; you really don't want to fall in love with a girl like me.
You will lose your faith.

When asked
"what is love?",
A little boy did a series of karate kicks.
And In my opinion,
that was the most honest answer
anyone's ever gave on that subject.

"I DIDN'T SEE LIFE GOING THIS WAY.
I OTHER PLANS YOU KNOW."

"LIKE WHAT?"

"LIKE NOT WANTING
TO GIVE UP EVERY DAY."

Insults

usually come from

those with dry salty throats

thirsty

for a sip of your lemonade.

Ya'll frontin'
Ya'll really don't love the poet.

You despise what it takes
to bring you this beautified pain.

Wanting the wine
Before we finish crushing the grapes.

They're wondering if she's a basket case.
She's just your Basquiat of today
Hitting you with unusual influential's
She's someone you have to adjust your mental to

They say I'm
Kanye West'ing
I embrace the refrence
They attack my preference
Too much confidence
It's so offensive.
They can't stand it.
It's too aggressive.
They can't handle it.

She's simply trying to live out her visions
They don't understand it.

DON'T LET SITUATIONS YOU CAN'T CONTROL,
CONTROL YOUR MIND
TO THE POINT YOU CAN'T CONTROL YOURSELF.

YOU'LL NEVER TRULY UNDERSTAND THE ARTIST.

THAT'S THE POINT.

He looked at her,
smiled,
and said...

"Will you be the one to drive me
crazy for the rest of my life?"

For he needed that,

To constantly be moved by a great force.

EVEN WHEN THE POET
IS ON THE OUT'S WITH LOVE ,
WE STILL HAVE TO MAKE SURE
YOU REMAIN
TOTALLY
IN LOVE.

Only 3 inches over 5 feet

But I always gotta be
the bigger person.

"I ain't even gonna lie...
She's not a good writer at all.
It's way worse than I thought..
She's an influential one.
You know what that means?"

"What?"

"You'll see."

SHE BROKE HIS HEART
AT LEAST ONCE A DAY.

HIS DAILY MEDICATION.

HEAVY DOSES
OF HEAVY EMOTIONS.

SHE WAS

THE POISON
THE ANTIDOTE
THE NAIL
THE ROPE
MISERY
AND
HOPE.

"POETS"

(LAUGHS)

"NOTHING BUT A BUNCH OF LOVERS
AT WAR WITH THEIR MADNESS."

THE ONLY THING YOU NEED TO PROVE

IS

YOU AIN'T LETTING THE MISERABLES GET THE BEST OF YOU.

How can one not go crazy living in this society?

SANE?

That's the luxurious life we're aiming for.

I don't take them seriously
if they haven't been floored before.

Crying on the floor.
Passed out on the floor.
Drunk on the floor.

In my book,
not experiencing those is a flaw.

I'mma think something is
definitely wrong wit ya.

SOME PEOPLE,
HARSH CRITICS;

BUT ASK TO SEE THEIR WORK,

CRICKETS

THE JONES' PLACE

Grass greener in the front yard...
And full of dead flowers in the backyard.

DO YOU WANT TO COME
LIVE IN A NEW
DIMENSION WITH ME.

WHY STAY HERE
WASTING OUR WILDEST
DREAMS ON THEIR
REALITY?

BUT KNOW IF YOU COME
WITH ME..
YOU'RE ALREADY IN TOO
DEEP

WINNIG CARD

I TOLD MYSELF THIS
YEAR
I WAS PULLING CARDS.
SO THE FIRST CARD I
PULLED WAS MINE.
IT WASN'T A QUEEN
IT WASN'T A KING
NOT A JACK OR AN ACE.
IT WAS A JOKER.
AND THAT'S WHEN I
KNEW ME BEING
DETRIMENTALLY NICE
WAS OVER.

12:22

On a frosty winter's night
I felt true love.
All it had to offer.
Transcendence.
A feeling beyond any profound description.
It was atonement for some of life's darkest days
As the sum of all things......
It was a gift of absolution sent from the universe.
I saw what I would have never seen in my craziest
dreams.
A feeling so ineffable.
Blanketing acoustics cascaded over my whole being,
leaving me floating in sound waves.
I was in a realm past the comprehension of genius
but shared the imagination station of an innocent
child.

It was true love.
I saw it.
I felt it.
I embraced it.
I reverenced it,
for it was benevolent.
Again, a feeling worth almost losing the fight against the world.

The feeling worth hearing the melancholic song I felt life composed on my behalf.
A feeling worth feeling the mercilessness of society and the incompatible relationship we had.
And even though it had crept up on me without caution,
in kindness it allowed me to feel its presence slip away,
slowly back into the abyss.

A procrastination that felt like the longest kiss goodbye.
And when it was gone, it was gone.
Just like that,
It was gone.

Let's fly high...er
it'll be mind blowing,
a big relief from...
mind controlling.
I'll keep your curiosity growing.
I'll keep your imagination flowing.
Keep you out there strolling through the
poppy fields
and onto
the yellow brick road.

LISTEN,
IT CAN ONLY GET BETTER
FROM HERE.
WE AIN'T GOT NO MONEY,
IN A CITY THAT AIN'T
CHEAP.
I KNOW SOME MIGHT SAY
WE'VE HIT ROCK BOTTOM .
BUT BABY,WE'RE AT
GROUND LEVEL.
AND THERE'S NOWHERE
TO GO BUT UP.

DON'T LOWER YOURSELF INTO
A BOTTOMLESS PIT OF LIES
TRYING TO KEEP SOMEONE IN
YOUR LIFE.
THEY'LL WATCH YOU TAKE THAT
TRIP,
KNOWING IT WILL LEAD TO YOUR
DEMISE.

JUMPING IN AND OUT
OF EMOTIONS LIKE
PARKOUR.
I'M SORRY
I KNOW THESE
FEELINGS ARE RAW.
I ONLY KNOW TO GIVE
YOU ALL OF THEM,
OR NONE AT ALL.

I rise in my power, not to overpower you,
but to EMPOWER you.

I merge with the pen and take you to another dimension.....
You ain't ever heard nothing like this....
You ain't ever seen nothing like this.....
They ain't ever said nothing like this....
They could never come close to it....
It ain't ever been this captivating
You won't ever have this experience again unless I provide the feeling.

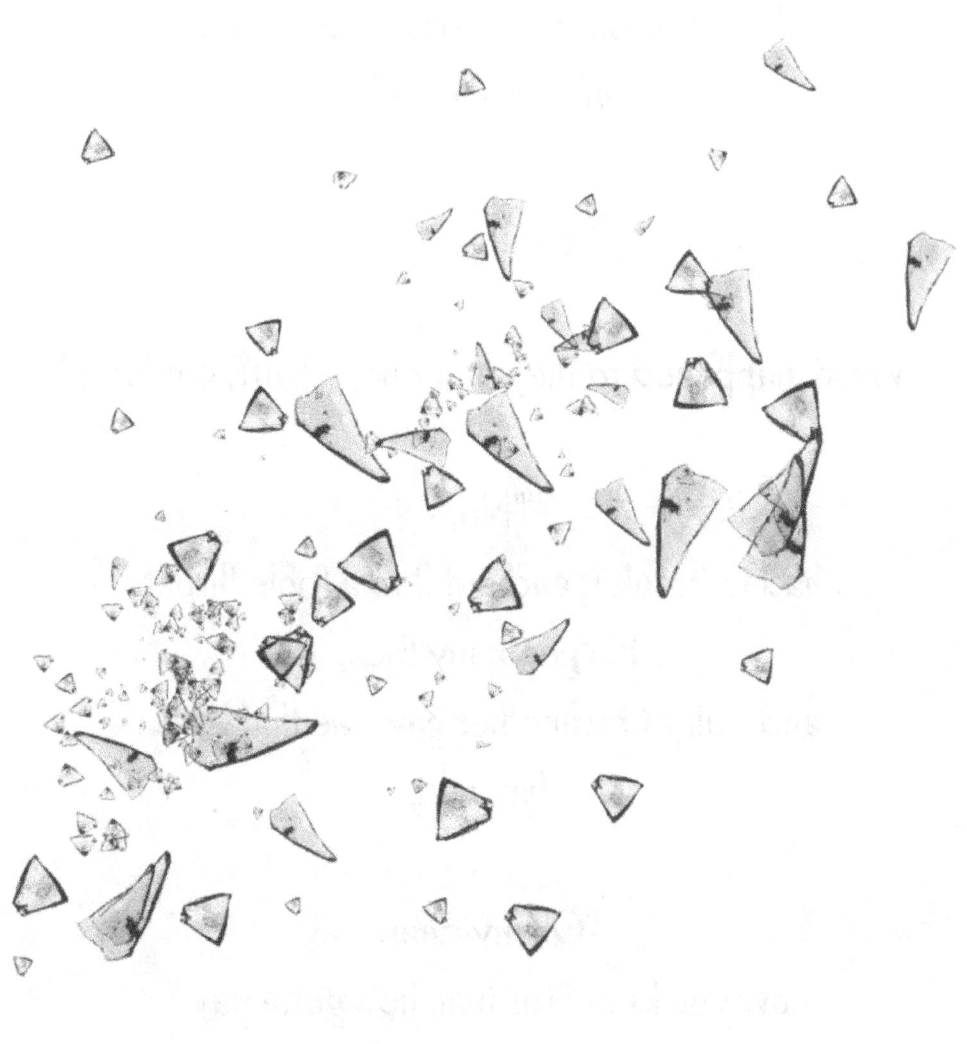

"Hey, you only have one glass slipper
in your closet."

"Yeah, I know."

"What happened to the other one, fell off, got lost?"

"No,
I had to break it and put it to a fools throat.
He got in my face,
and Fairy Godmother gave me that look
that said,

"Oh my dear,
now you know for that, he's gotta pay."

PLEEEEEASE,
KEEP THEM TALKING.
LET ALL THAT HOT AIR
BLOW YOUR SAILS.

YELLOW BRICK ROAD

Down the yellow brick road,
imagine the stories told.
Imagine the secrets
those bricks hold.
Dreamers on the
golden journey,
on the path
to realize
that their mind
is a goldmine.

☆☆☆

See,

don't wory about how your story is being told.

The story always changes, the more people tell it.

Details get added and subtracted, the worst gets the most attention, and the good somehow becomes faded memories.

It's the synopsis of your story that they can't change.

It's just telling how you went for the gold by obliterating the obstacles along the road.

So let them talk that talk,

while you walk that walk.

☆☆☆

YOU WEREN'T DESIGNED TO FUNCTION PROPERLY IN A WORLD THAT WAS DESIGNED FOR YOU TO FAIL.

GO WHERE THE
"CRAZIES"
ARE.

THERE.
YOU'LL FIND THE TRUTH.

It's THEM vs. US
the bullshit, we wont let it immerse us,
We've been sold too many lies.
Time to reimburse trust.
Surfs up, we've all cried rivers.
This shits a circus.
We out here with our fists up,
they let us down then say
" keep your chin up".
They'll eat us for dinner.
Put us against each other,
then say it's the battle of the saint vs. the sinner
It's so much to be taught ,
remember you're still a beginner.
It's time to return what we've bought back to sender.
Rearrange the agenda.
With all our pent up anger, it's time to persecute the offenders,
and praise the avenger.

SELF LOVE
WILL PULL YOU UP FROM DROWNING IN A SEA OF
REGRETS.

REMEMBER,
NO ONE IS PERFECT,

IF YOU'RE NOT OUT HERE CAUSING HAVOC IN OTHERS LIVES,
THEN YOU ARE DOING EXCELLENT.

DONT LET
"KNOW IT ALLS"
CONFUSE YOU.
THEY HARDLY KNOW WHAT'S BEST FOR THEM
SO KNOW
THEY DON'T KNOW WHAT'S BEST FOR YOU.

WE'LL TALK AGAIN SOON

www.ingramcontent.com/pod-product-compliance
Lightning Source LLC
LaVergne TN
LVHW050321160826
845677LV00014B/3504

* 9 7 9 8 3 5 5 0 1 0 2 9 4 *